The Homing Bird

Bashabi Fraser

Indigo Dreams Publishing

First Edition: The Homing Bird
First published in Great Britain in 2017 by:
Indigo Scotland
24 Forest Houses
Halwill
Beaworthy
EX21 5UU
www.indigodreams.co.uk

Indigo Scotland is an imprint of Indigo Dreams Publishing Ltd.
Bashabi Fraser has asserted her right under the Copyright,
Designs and Patents Act 1988 to be identified as the author of
this work.

ISBN 978-1-910834-34-3

British Library Cataloguing in Publication Data. A CIP record
for this book can be obtained from the British Library.

Designed and typeset in Palatino Linotype by Indigo Dreams.
Cover design by Ronnie Goodyer at Indigo Dreams.
Author photograph by Kingshuk Bhattacharya.
Printed and bound in Great Britain by: 4edge Ltd
www.4edge.co.uk

Papers used by Indigo Dreams are recyclable products made
from wood grown in sustainable forests following the guidance
of the Forest Stewardship Council.

Acknowledgements

I would like to thank the following journals/books for publishing some of the poems that have been put together in this pamphlet : *Home Thoughts : Poetry of the British Indian Diaspora* (Allahabad, India: Cyberwit.net, 2016), *Breaking the Mould: Edinburgh: Researching and Celebrating 100 years of Women's History in Social and Political Activism since the beginning of WW1*, (Workers Educational Association, Scotland, 2015), *Episteme* (June 2015, Vol 4/1), *Muse India* (Issue 56, July-Aug, 2014), *The Statesman Festival Issue* (Kolkata, 2014), *Bengal Partition Stories : An Unclosed Chapter* (London : Anthem Press, 2006, 2008).

CONTENTS

The Homing Bird

Part I
Kolkata

Kolkata do you miss me?
As your eleven million surged to
Sixteen, did your avenues
And alleys and crossings
Turn every corner, scour
The pavements and follow
The mounting skyline – looking
For me? As your electric trains
Brought thousands everyday
And spilt them like lentils
Scuttling across market spaces,
Entering your factories, shops,
And kitchens, did you
Ever stop for breath, to
Steal a moment of calm
To think of me? Do you
Remember my little face
Caressed by the trellis
Of your balconies, entranced
By the spouting fountain
Of your 6 o'clock hydrants?
Do you remember your Maidan[1] mists
The taste of your burnt clay
Cha cloying my morning outings
As the chawallah was swallowed
By the mysterious fronds
Of haze that sinuously wound round
Victoria Memorial and St Paul's Cathedral?

---

[1] A park like the Meadows, called the green lung of Kolkata.

Kolkata – you were my city
Where colourful kites on armoured
Strings vied with birds of prey,
And terraces met like beehives
Of open activity – a gigantic
Tenement with the roof removed
To communicate as one community.
Kolkata, you were mine to play in,
To duck behind the potted flowers
Of St James Park or immerse myself
In the immensity of Park Circus
Maidan, crying to the descending dusk
Once when I was lost as a toddler,
And trembling on the breast of my
Seeking aunt who embraced me
with sobbing relief - just like you
Kolkata, the city where my parents
Found a home when a frontier
Appeared like a weeping barricade
Between what had been theirs
And now had to be fabricated
Amidst your intimate streets
For thousands like them, who
Had left their all for your city walls –
Not out of curiosity but by the whims
Of time that drove them at the stroke
Of midnight from a known history
To an unknown struggle born of
A one-man commission, cutting
A nation with a knife-edged pen
In the privacy of his room.
So Kolkata, you became my parents'
City in a forced marriage with
A bride they grew to love from
The moment you made it clear that
You were the matriarch who had opened

Your portals to the deluge that poured
Into your depthless depths of generous
Immensity. They were your *ghar jamai*[2]
The grooms who had sought your shelter,
And switched loyalties from the sheer fear
Of being left destitute for being
On the 'wrong side' of a border
They had neither created nor longed for.
So Kolkata, you became a haven
For the bereft and bereaved,
The city of migrants. Enfolding new
Dialects within your old quilted
Network of cosmopolitan reality
Of Parsis and Iranians,
Anglo-Indians and Armenians,
The spicy twangs from Marwar, Punjab,
Tamil Nadu and Kerala,
And then confronted with the flavour
Of tones and accents from the breast
Of the riverine districts
Across Mymensingh, Barishal,
Chittagong and Sylhet[3] –
Gushing like so many tributaries
To swell and augment your existing
Bengali with the new experience
Of displacement and loss, encountering
The agitation of mobilizing missions,
Land grabbing commissions,
Squatters' colonies and demonstrations,
And long-drawn-out law-suits that
Gave your courts a Dickensian aura
Of Chancery with their delaying tactics

---

[2] Husbands who decide to stay in their in-laws' house.
[3] Districts which were part of undivided Bengal and after
Partition, became part of East Pakistan (now Bangladesh).

Played out in your Gothic
High Court, redolent of the Raj
As your Square which you reclaimed
From Dalhousie in your renaming programme,
Where I have queued for minibuses
Hopped onto circulating trams
And braved the mid-day sun
To register a parcel at GPO[4],
Book a sleeper at Fairlie Place
Or satisfy the secret code answer
To the white uniformed guard
At Writers Building, from where
Your populace's fate is decided
By thousands of tea-sipping,
Newspaper-reading bureaucrats
Who were deeply attached to that
Vanishing tribe of old typewriters,
Committed to the nostalgic grip
Of red-tape that will not let go
Its hold on you, just as you hold us
In your hypnotic grasp of open-armed intimacy.
Here on your streets, Kolkata,
I have walked till my frail sandals snapped
And always found a deft cobbler
Willing to mend soles and straps
Just as you put together broken families
And hearts scavenging your pavements
To find means of putting body and soul together,
Cramped like knotted intestines in the bowels
Of your crowded houses, like too many teeth
In a young woman's ageing mouth,
Lining your lanes and alleyways
That have always beamed alive
As your city streets stirred

---

[4] The General Post Office.

With smoking coal stoves
Hours before dawn broke
And puffy eyes blinked
On another long day of valorous survival
From pallet beds, woken from a few hours
Of sleep stolen as your houses slept
Kolkata, while the embers smouldered
Between your dreams and your formidable reality.

It is here that I have seen your rickshaw wallahs
Stretch their reluctant joints that had not quite rested
From their previous day's agony and aches
As they braced their *lungis*[5] in a fresh, spruce knot,
Their dignity salvaged, their tiredness reprieved
With the giving water of your municipal hydrants
Kolkata, as you sent their bells clinking
Along your waking streets, that remnant of bondage
And embarrassing labour, a burden of the past
That has been rivalled by mad minibuses
Who wear the colour that drives the bulls mad
As they crash through milling crowds
Who part like the Jordan for these new gods,
Challenged only by a lesser one –
The cheeky auto rickshaw[6] that squeals
Like scurrying three legged rats through imagined gaps,
Ideal for your 6% road surface area, an absurd,
Inadequate network for your mammoth sprawl –
Kolkata, that was once the second city of Empire
With your palaces along the dreaming river,
Your splurging jute mills and sprawling bungalows,
The green heart in your Maidan
Where horses sped with polo riders

---

5 A sarong which men wear in India.
6 A motorised rickshaw with three wheels which operates like a
taxi in Indian cities.

Watched by the white town
At Chowringhee, while the black town grew
In a mangle of problematic capillaries,
Unsupervised but magnetic as it drew
The ambitious and aspiring from rural holdings
Of Bengal, the blazing deserts of Rajasthan and
The central plains of India - to your markets
And your port, your cosmopolitan hub of activity
– A city of contrasting histories –
A prison for the Nawabs
A fort for the conquerors –
Do you remember each epoch
As one scroll was wrapped up
And put away and another unfurled
To record what you witnessed, Kolkata,
As ships docked and sailed from your harbour,
Attracting diverse nations to collide
Against the murky Hugli, betting at the races,
While golfers teed off at the Tolly[7],
The dewy blades suppliant
To their exclusive club camaraderie
Till you became the City of Clubs,
The Calcutta rivalling the Bengal,
The Lake and Rowing Clubs[8] contemplating
The mirrored green of Dhakuria Lakes,
As brown men chalked out fresh spaces
Or found themselves occupants of old edifices
When one era elapsed at the
Stroke of midnight and another began…

---

[7] Tollygunge Club.
[8] Indians were not allowed into The Bengal Club, which is why
they set up the Calcutta Club. The Lake Club and Rowing Club
were established for rowers and are now welcoming spaces to
entertain family and friends.

Part II
Edinburgh

And I was one of those post-midnight children
Who grew up with the tales of the 'other' nation
Beyond an uncrossable line of nostalgic distance,
Signifying my grandmother's blushing bridehood
And my parents' childhood of paddy field plenty –
From which I turned to Kolkata's track-bound trams
And sky-free pigeons for my vision of possible flights –
Which came years later, pursuing ambitions
Floated by ship escapes to the island
That resembled Dalhousie Square magnified,
And Ballygunge bungalows lined in neat rows
But double-deckered to match its ubiquitous red buses.

You were my student city Edinburgh, where bus fares
Were beyond my affordable dreams,
So I chose to walk, not in delicate sandals
But sturdy boots that marked the pavements
Of this walkable Athens of the North,
As the familiar buses sauntered by,
Coursing through each of my cities.

So I crossed and recrossed the oceans, churning the depths
For memories that followed me in exploring shoals
Till I came to stay in the city where
I learnt to drive according to set rules,
Safe from the aggressive chaos of a motley crowd
Of wheeled citizens locked in a competition
To outwit and outspeed each other in Kolkata's
Undaunted sprawl –

Here, where wide avenues have
Marked lanes to protect my progress,
I have witnessed a similar upheaval as dreamlines

Have been invoked in a muddle that has baffled
Us everyday in old arteries being blocked
While fresh capillaries appear
As Edinburgh made ready for a tramline
To slow down its pace and save its northern air
With the breathing relic of its imperial heyday.
It is like a silent film replayed as months
Of madness that made hills sprout in the Maidan
When the metro was the excuse for organized chaos
In my old city, now transferred to the knotted
Reality of Leith Walk and Shandwick Place,
In my chosen dwelling space.

And now the gleaming white trams weave with confidence
Down Princes Street where people meet in this intimate city.

So my pace has changed as I embrace
Edinburgh, exchanging tropical abandon
For temperate caution, adjusting my lens
From streets that sagged with the weight of a populace
To wonder where the people have all gone
In Edinburgh, watching the same double-deckers
That light-tread with elegance here, allowing a view
Through its unhindered windows –
So unlike the tilting pensioners
Cruising with the burden of hanging commuters
Clinging like a desperate litter
To a mother cat's sagging tits.

My arrival has been nondescript.
I have come back to you Edinburgh, without fanfare
Of welcome. Your trees were listless
And the Meadows slept, while your wind
Unfolded my sari, which I put away
To enter your storyline in colours you accept –
But have you accepted me, Edinburgh?

You are no stranger to me, for I know
Your wynds and crescents, each curious close,
Your basalt rock and Forth view.

I have been drenched by the invisible drizzle
Of your *haars*[9]. I have pirouetted
With my gambolling umbrella at the DHT[10] steps,
And it is here, watched by Scott and Hume
With their open books, that I have opened
My pages to the world, in this City of Literature,
Where Rebus frowns through Flesh Market Close
And Hogwarts looms in the many-towered splendour
Of George Heriot's School, where
My daughter was an inmate, sharing
The magic of its quadrangular secrets.
You remain, Edinburgh, the urban inspiration
Of Geddesian vision and a Makar's[11] delight.

But will you let me blend in Edinburgh
With the flowing pen power you hold in your folds?
Can the Stanzas of your many steps
Divide to let my lines interstice your spaces –
Edinburgh? Are your stone tenements
The embodiment of strength, their cold surface
Belying their warm interior of ensconcing intent?

---

[9] The *haar* is formed over the sea and is carried to coastal areas by the wind. It is like a light, incessant drizzle, a coastal fog with a misty mysteriousness that is quite common in Edinburgh.
[10] David Hume Tower is a tall building in the George Square campus of Edinburgh University. The steps leading up to it and the courtyard outside it, form one of the windiest parts of Edinburgh.
[11] A Scots word for a poet/bard.

When I walk through the Grassmarket,
Gaze up from Johnstone Terrace as the one o'clock gun
Startles me and the terrier across on Granny's Steps,
Will you mistake me for a visitor,
Taking in the sites? Will you let your eyes
Slide over me, or will you, Edinburgh, linger with me
As I trudge up Calton Hill for a picture postcard
View of Princes Street and will you stand by my side,
Agreeing that there is no need to hurry away,
For this is where I've come to stay
And from your vantage point, I can rain
My thoughts in celebratory confetti
Over this city, to merge with its cloud canopy
And dissolve with its rare sunlight,
Suffusing my lines with the skyline of Edinburgh.

Anchoring Aesthetics

to the Bengali Cultural Association: East of Scotland

The wind on my back
Propelled me to this shore
Where the snowdrifts swirled
Around me in this city I had known before.

It was here and from across
The Forth – the dreaming Kingdom of Fife
That I picked up fragments
And reminiscences of a distant life

That I had left behind.
And you brought a prized ship
To my door, docking at my shore
With a cargo of warm friendship

Sweetened by *sandesh*[12] and *payesh*[13]
Savouried by choice fish dishes
Made mellifluous by Tagore and Nuzrul's
Songs, spiced auspiciously by good wishes

Of a community that met to create
Through the dancing rhythms of time
That have anchored me in my youth
And replenished me in my prime.

---

[12] A delicate Bengali sweet made from cottage cheese.
[13] Bengali rice pudding flavoured with green cardamom and
bay leaves.

This Border

There was a time when you and I
Chased the same butterfly
Climbed the same stolid trees
With the fearless expertise
That children take for granted
Before their faith is stunted

Do you remember how we balanced a wheel
Down dusty paths with childish zeal
Do you remember the ripples that shivered
As we ducked and dived in our river
Do you remember what we shared
Of love and meals, and all we dared
Together – without fears
Because we were one
In those past years
Before we knew that butterflies
Were free to share our separate skies
That they could cross with graceful ease
To alight on stationary trees
On either side of this strange line
That separates yours from mine
For whose existence we rely
Entirely on our inward eye
This border by whose callous side
Our inert wheel lies stultified
This border that cuts like a knife
Through the waters of our life
Slicing fluid rivers with
The absurdity of a new myth
That denies centuries
Of friendships and families
This border that now decrees
One shared past with two histories

This border that now decides
The sky between us as two skies
This border born of blood spilt free
Makes *you* my friend, my enemy.

Walled-In : Walled-Out

Do good walls make good neighbours?
And what is good about walls unless
They belong to my home
And cocoon me in against the elements,
Keeping me storm-free or unscorched,
Blanketed and private –
A space for me with my family,
Walls that stand between dignity
And life on the pavement.

But stand them up to embody
The shadow line of a political border
Something that signifies the Other
As the intruder –
Walls that form the rampart
Of empire, of cold war, of occupation –
And create the enemy
Who is shut out, and cannot,
And definitely should not, impregnate it,
Shell it, crack it or cross it
Even if his brother lives,
Or his farmland lies, or his mother's grave,
And his fishing river and playmate tree
Exist beyond what he must see
As the territory of his enemy.

So while walls shut out
Suicide bombers, harvesters, employees
Of the starving free, they shut in
The waller who cements fear
In brick and stone, in suspicion born
Of segregation that grows
Without association with the Other –
The unknown face of the foe

Which, if he had known
Could remove walls from minds
Discovering bonds in human kind
Instead of building terror zones.

This Difference

The difference between you and me
Has been carefully architectured in the segments
Of your imagination.

For centuries we bartered amicably
We cultivated, irrigated, constructed
Without enflaming friction.

Then the competition began for opportunities
That were not enough for our sharply
Growing population.

It was then that you built your raging kiln
And shaped each brick with putty questionability
In your conflagration.

Piling up brick on brick to form a scalding wall
Between us, each grain coerced together by hate
And upheld by a conviction

That has driven me to a land I didn't know,
To rivers I had never set my boat afloat in –
In another nation.

You can take the house I was born in
The roads I walked, the crops I grew
And deny my education.

You can tell me I do not belong with yours
That you and I were never friends in our years
Of subtle integration.

You can divide lands, houses, forests, people,
Mountains, lakes, roads and jobs
Through lines of interpretation –

Lines that carve up rooms and fields
And create blocks, invisible but true
Only in your imagination.

And when you try to harness streams
And split the sky to nurture dreams
Of absurd divisions –

You forget that nature deems each effort
Of your futile greed to allocate, as an interruption
To her continuation.

And with nature my mind flies
To invade your precious guarded skies
With renewed determination.

You cannot take what lives in me
Of nostalgia and memory,
You cannot make me settle down
In this town that's not my own.

And how will we now decide
To call our own and divide
Our literature, our arts and songs,
Our rituals round what's right and wrong?

But in the world's fair scrutiny
Whenever they see you and me,
They cannot see this difference
That we have built through inference.

India Calls

Wave on wave of humanity rolled
Through her mountain passes
Boat after boat arrived
At her ample, open shores.
Her lap was large, her cradle soft
Her arms were bountiful with gifts –
They came to take, they came for more
There was no dearth to her rich store
They loved her for her growing plains,
Expansive, fertile and well-drained.
Some returned, most came to stay
Adopting her appealing ways
Blood mingled with blood to form
This multi-ethnic vast nation
An unparalleled diversity
In paradoxical proximity
Of melting snows on mountain tops
And arid lands and thriving crops
Watched by blue eyes' startling hue
Matched by auburn curls of few
While raven locks adorn and crown
White and black toned down to brown
Her demographic clock ticks merrily on
She stands strong, past one billion
Five thousand years she has survived,
Post-empire, severed[14], she thrives
The old sits smugly with the new
Industrial smoke with the humble hoe
Spires, minarets and domes
Huts beside the rich men's homes
The Ambassador[15] still going strong

---

[14] India was partitioned at the time of her Independence in 1947, to form Pakistan.

While Indicas[16] now join the throng
Double-deckers veer away
From autos'[17] ubiquitous sway
Battery run television sets
Where electric lines don't penetrate
Kurtas vie with collared shirts
And saris rival mini skirts
The slow, sagacious bullock carts
Ambling past plush cyber marts –
So just as strangers joined the fold
New trends don't replace the old
The world has moved in once again
Calling her in her domain[18].

---

[15] The Ambassador car is a bigger version of the old Morris
Minor, made by Hindustan Motors, whose sturdy make adapts
well to Indian roads.
[16] The Indica is a car made by Tata – modern, well-regarded and
popular.
[17] Auto-rickshaws are three-wheelers with diesel engines,
driven recklessly and aggressively through traffic jams; a
popular mode of transport operating like taxis in towns and
cities of the sub-continent.
[18] A reference to the Call Centres of multinational companies in
India.

In my India

In the India that I knew
My mother met my father
In the portals of knowledge
Debated freely while their
Coffee grew cold under the
Noisy fans of the Coffee House.

In my India my parents
Married across caste
Norms, accepted by both
Families – my mother for her
Grace and mellifluous voice
My father for his gentleness and brilliance.

In the India that I knew
I was valued as a girl
In my extended family
Who glowed at every dance drama
I choreographed and performed.

In my India my intrepid
Mother could rush out
Of her university classroom
To stop a vast crowd of students
From political campaigning in her domain

In the India that I knew
My father could confront
A police force intent on
Arresting Naxalites from
The Student Halls on the university campus.

In my India my Brahmin
Father, displaced by Partition

Could employ a Muslim cook
And my mother leave me in
The care of Amina's mother –
Our devoted matriarchs.

In the India that I knew
A girl molested on a bus
Would have the conductor
And driver and a whole
Angry crowd protecting her dignity.

In the India that I loved
I could cycle through a forest
Walk back alone as dawn
Broke after a sitar concert
The Bhairav following my footsteps.

In the India where my youth
Blossomed, young men made
Witty remarks that made us blush
With pleasure as we walked past,
Basking in the admiration of their glance.

In my India we danced
At Holi, ate biryani at Eid
Watched a thousand lamps
Shine at Buddha Purnima, lit
Candles at Easter, and had a roast dinner
Watched by a resplendent Christmas tree.

In the India that I knew
We believed that education
Was a tool the caste-born and
Caste-less, the displaced and dispossessed
Could use to sharpen their reason and prosper.

In my India politics was about
A land reform movement,
About better distribution,
About social service, about destroying
Corruption by dreaming idealists.

In the India that I knew
No one told me what to wear,
What to practise, what to eat
Whom to marry, whom to claim
As my friend, companion, colleague and neighbour.

In my India we were moving
With the world, pushing orthodox
Boundaries, countering ignorance
In the Spirit of Rabindranath
In tune with Gandhiji's tolerance.

In my India we were modern
We nurtured the petals of culture
We were sustained by creativity
We revered our grandmothers
And mothers who had won our
Freedoms for us, opening India's door wide.

Give me back *my* India!

Fog on Hill Cart Road
(between Darjeeling and Siliguri)

It was the same fog
That heavy treaded
Down the mountains
Slurping round
The shadowy bends
Its black humour
Gleefully revealed
In lurching
Threats to throw
Us over its
Shoulder, down
The slope
That deft
Nepali drivers
Avoided
With the skill
Of the blind,
More wily
Than the pall
From hell.

Fog on M8
(between Glasgow and Edinburgh)

It came without warning
A pall that covered all –
The dunnest blanket
From hell.
The road disappeared
And in its place
An awning spurting
Cold smoke –
Slithering tongues
From a demonic
Cauldron.
If you listened
You could hear
Sinister notes
Curling round
Shadowy presences.
We slow paced
In a funeral march
The brake lights
Of a coffin ahead
Our only guide.

Christmas: Burra Deen

We had turned from the white streets of London
From carol singing on a wintry afternoon
The snowman looking up to admire
The glinting Christmas tree at the window –
To reflective blue skies
A warm wrap-around sun of fun
And of trees with paper leaves
Cut into frills of fir foliage, defying
The ambient green branches and colourful
Butterfly hues on bushes redolent
Of colonial migrations of dahlias,
Cosmos, petunias, poppies and
Chrysanthemums in white plenitude
Snow-like on a soft Christmas night.
We had picked a sparkling star
Of Bethlehem to hang at our window
A nativity scene in clay, tinsel streamers
And holly that didn't quite look like holly
In its plasticky obviousness
From New Market's grand arcades
Which Hogg Saheb had built in Calcutta.
We had come home with Dundee cake in
A round tin, with sweet aromatic
Darjeeling oranges, to supplement
Ma's homemade fruit cake, her
Bengali Bhetki fries
Her roast chicken, subtly spiced cauliflower
And peppered potatoes tumbled in ghee
That we ate before the Christian millions
Set out to sing carols in India's churches
At Midnight Mass, and the nation slept
To wake up on a national holiday
On Burra Deen – the Big Day of Christmas.

The Midnight Calls

When the fingers of the night curl around
One half of the reeling globe
Enwrapping supine souls in told dreams,
Some lie awake, having travelled
From the other part, physically here
While their thoughts dare jet miles
And enter the sun swathed world
Of those they left behind,
Reliving their every irksome chore,
Their compulsive duties, their age-weary moments,
While the would-be sleeper's reluctant ear is half alert
Fearing those midnight and small hour calls
'Hello... hello... yes, I can hear you
Can you hear me? Is everything all right
What... what has happened... when?'
Expectant, yet not welcoming the news,
Knowing each interruption, each intrusion
Is a message of another departure
As one more name is struck off
The phone book, not to be reached
Again in long-distance voice links
Though remembered in a smile
And a sense of comfort
That will remain amidst a consciousness
Of a void, as part of a life that is not yet
Buried under an archaeological pile
Of forgotten histories.

Cricket – Eastern Style

When the soft winter sun
Wraps everyone
In a siesta of dreams
They stay in the streets
In their brown bare feet
And play like kings.

Their bat is a plank
Their ball a castaway
Their wickets are drawn
On a wall at the back
Of any alleyway
Far from green lawns.

They are the batsmen
Of the future
Scoring centuries
They are off-spinners
Of some stature
Bowling victories.

Cricket in Sussex

Applause startles the snoozing poodle dreaming
On Sussex's sunny Downs
The whizzing ball cheekily claiming a boundary
Where there are no boundaries
The batsmen watch with satisfaction
They who traverse England and India
With ease, playing in dusty cities there
Happy to challenge the green here
On a rare summer day.

Home

It has always been the same, the garden path awash
With snow-like chrysanthemums caressing my walk
The veranda embraced by the interlaced abundance
Of dark green with purple clusters dripping from stalks

Which beckoned a cycle of life, fluttering,
Hovering and crawling through its myriad folds.
Inside are muralled walls where peacocks dance
Surrounded by more tendrils etched in gold

Our Marshall cat on watch, the parrots upside down
Nibbling plump guavas with genteel grace, guests who
Fly back in green clouds at dusk to their forest home
While my mother welcomes other guests through

Her open door. It has always been so in my dreams when
She was there, before the creepers came cascading in.

Indigo Dreams Publishing Ltd
24, Forest Houses
Cookworthy Moor
Halwill
Beaworthy
Devon
EX21 5UU
www.indigodreams.co.uk